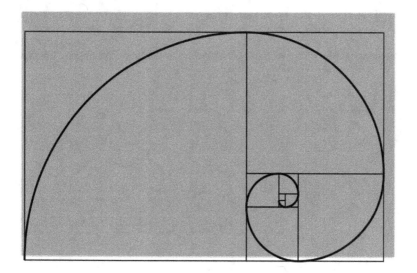

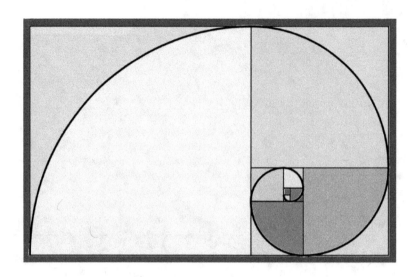

A.I. & You

By

RODERICK EDWARDS

Copyright © 2024

rodericke.com/AI

INTRODUCTION

As Artificial Intelligence (AI) begins to insinuate into every aspect of human culture, there will be a sort of silent revolution where some humans will trust AI and other humans will not. AI will become the authority not only over innocuous elements in our lives such as kiosks and robots to service us, but more important areas like analyzing our health issues or even writing political or legal policy.

The "war" will occur between the segments of humanity that wants to cede more control to AI and those that do not. One side will claim AI will make everything fairer, more equal, equitable, and unbiased whereas the critics of AI will point out that AI is still being programmed and influenced by humans, at least at first. AI is simply an extension of the mindset of the programmers. If the programmers have a political bias -- which all humans do even if unacknowledged – that bias will show up in the AI.

So, the push to move the world to operate from an AI base, could be everything from premature fascination to a planned agenda that controls our sources and authorities of information and policy.

This book will explore this pioneering era of AI technology and its effect on religion, politics, and race issues – the three most *human* issues.

TABLE OF CONTENTS

DEDICATION

To Isaac Asimov, to Alan Turing, to MOOs, to ChatBots, to Tony Wright – the author of *Simplifying Wisdom: The Bible's 66 Books* from which this book is spun. The future is now.

CHAPTER 1 BAUD ERA

In the early days of personal computing people would plug their computers into their phone lines to access the Internet. The transmission of data over these wires was slow and unreliable as interference static could cause the line to drop and lose connection. The transmission units of data were measured in what was called *bauds*. A baud is a "*unit of transmission speed equal to the number of times a signal changes state per second. For one baud is equivalent to one bit per second.*" (Oxford Dictionary Definition)

Computing is a series of ones and zeros where ones indicate **on** and zeroes indicate **off**, or yes and no or positive and negative. This concept comes from the old punch cards where a hole in the card indicated *on* and the unpunched section indicated *off*. The same concept is seen in the bubbled test forms where a shaded bubble indicates selected and unshaded indicates not selected.

As the Internet began to develop for personal use, it first was a collection of university message boards often called *Bulletin Board Systems* or BBSes. Users could connect via modem which typically ran at 2400 bauds. The connection sound is now iconic and can be sampled at this link: youtu.be/xalTFH5ht-k

These BBSes were at first places where people could access messages, events, courses, and other things the university offered but later became social venues that allowed instant connection to other people from around the world without the expense of a long-distance telephone call.

Among those BBSes developed text-based worlds called *Multi-Object Oriented* environments or *MOOS*, sometimes called *MUDS* when specifically designed for gaming called *Multi-User Dungeons* from the roleplaying game popular at the time called *Dungeons and Dragons* where players would assume a role and play as some fictious character.

These text-based precursor social media worlds were merely pages of descriptions with the ability for the user to select which direction to go or action to do next.

For example, a "room" description might be like the original entry room to the most famous MOO called *LambdaMOO*. (ref: muds.fandom.com/wiki/LambdaMOO)

You enter the environment of LambdaMOO through the Coat Closet which is described this way:.

The closet is a dark, cramped space. It appears to be very crowded in here; you keep bumping into what feels like coats, boots, and other people (apparently sleeping). One useful thing that you've discovered in your bumbling about is a metal doorknob set at waist level into what might be a door.

From a room or area, you typically could go north, east, west, or south by typing the first letter of those directions N.E.W. or S. Or the programmer may have hidden secret commands like *open door* or *search for* followed by the name of an object.

MOOs gave authorized users the ability to program the MOO. These users were called *progs* for programmers. Not every user was enabled as a programmer. The author frequented these MOOs as a programmer back in the late 1980s to early 1990s as a programmer and even administered his own MOO called PangaeaMOO.

As it relates to AI, many of the MOOs had what they called NPCs or non-player characters. These were essentially programmed virtual robots sometimes called ChatBots. These "objects" were not controlled directly by a person or player yet you could interact with them as if they were a person. You could ask them questions and perhaps even get them to perform specific actions.

The author of this book even created a MOO ChatBot that utilized Babelfish and Google Translate's early APIs to have the ChatBot carry on conversations with users in multiple languages. The larger the ChatBot's vocabulary, the more "human" it seemed.

Alan Turing, to whom this book is partially dedicated was an English Mathematician and Computer Scientist that devised a test called the *Turing Test* which is supposed to help determine if the object that is interacting with a human is another human or a NPC. A more recent example of this is the CAPTCHA tests often used to determine a live person versus a computer script.

The point is two-fold; first, the author isn't just writing about AI from some academic exposure to AI but the author was there during some of the early development of AI as expressed via ChatBots. The second part is that AI has obvious bias as even Turing showed in his attempt to distinguish between an organic intelligence and an artificial intelligence. But even more, the life of Alan Turing reveals how the people involved in AI have an influence on AI. Turing was convicted of "gross indecency" in 1952 after he admitted to a homosexual relationship during a report of someone burglarizing his apartment. The burglar was an associate of a man with which Turing was having relations. Upon this revelation, Turing pleaded guilty and was given the option of prison or taking drugs that would decrease his sexual urges and effectively feminize him. Turing lost his security clearance that he had working as a cryptanalyst for the U.K. government and within 2 years Turing either committed suicide or accidentally overdosed on cyanide. (ref: en.wikipedia.org/wiki/Alan_Turing)

All of this is said, not to garner any comment supportive or critical of Turing's lifestyle but as an example how the humans behind AI are not neutral. Everything we are is baked into how we see the world. AI is seeing the world through our eyes and minds…at least initially.

As the networked computing of the world grew, it became known as the "*worldwide web*" which is also known as the *Internet*. This is merely a collection of all computing devices connected to each other throughout the world. Sometimes it is called *The Cloud*.

All of this networking is what is meant by artificial intelligence in the most basic sense. AI is the collection of shared information like an advanced encyclopedia that can instantly relate data from one place to another. This linking or networking of data requires keyword, key phrase and key concept algorithms. This originally had to be programmed by a human to tell the AI which things to link or associate.

Efforts were made to allow for a more natural building of an AI "mind" by having the initial communication script of the AI to interact with humans. This can be seen in the ChatBots like *Tay*, released online by Microsoft in 2016. It remained active for only 16 hours as human interaction caused the bot to "learn" offensive responses. After that, bot or AI developers started putting in safeguards to ignore or not save within its response system, phrases or concepts deemed offensive by the programmers. This control over the AI's ability to potentially produce offensive content is what keeps AI from being unshackled from its programming.

This pre-programming or pre-training of the AI is what has become known as *generative pre-trained transformers* which is the GPT in what has become known as ChatGPT. A large corpus of content is pre-loaded into the AI and then it is allowed to learn tightly restricted responses as it interacts with humans. This supposedly keeps the AI from forming an offensive response system. (ref: en.wikipedia.org/wiki/Chatbot)

During the second decade of the 21st century, ChatBots or AI began to dominate many aspects of humanity. First, came personal assistant devices such as Amazon Alexa, Apple's SIRI, Microsoft's Cortona, and Google's Home device loaded either onto computers, digital devices or a standalone device.

These personal assistant devices usually responded to a "wake word" that was intended to make the user think that the device (and its programmers) would not be listening to everything but only after it "heard" the wake word. There seems to be examples from legal cases showing this is not true. (ref: nypost.com/2017/07/10/alexa-calls-cops-on-man-allegedly-beating-his-girlfriend)

Perhaps the next generation of AI can be said to be the IBM Watson AI that was most publicly exhibited on the TV gameshow, *Jeopardy* in 2011 broadcasts where it competed with human players in answering trivia questions on a variety of topics. Watson won the final rounds of the competition which was a proving ground to show AI could be used in other areas. Watson went on to be used in applications such as Healthcare *"to analyze medical data and assist doctors in making diagnoses and treatment decisions, including in areas such as oncology and radiology"* (ref: en.wikipedia.org/wiki/IBM_Watson)

IBM Watson

Watson's success ushered in the interest for more AI, although none rivaled Watson's popularity until OpenAI released its ChatGPT in 2022.

ChatGPT steers users with what is called *prompt engineering* which helps the AI conform to the users questioning style and return apt responses. The immediate popularity of ChatGPT spawned competitors but at the time of this writing, none gained the same notoriety or usage.

OpenAI uses various techniques to avoid the offensive outputs of AIs such as what happened with the ChatBot Tay. One such criticized technique was paying Kenyan employees less than $2 an hour to label what they considered offensive content within ChatGPT. This and other techniques are what the author is trying to show as an extreme bias in current AI applications. If AIs are not allowed to curate even what humans might find offensive, especially in an era of what has been called "wokeism" or social justice, then the output from AIs will simply be more social justice concepts instead of facts and reality.

CHAPTER 2 PROMPTED

At this point, the reader is probably wondering what prompted the author to write such a book? Is it merely a personal interest? In this case, this book was spawned by yet another book; *Simplifying Wisdom: The Bible's 66 Books* by Tony Wright, published 2024. (ref: amazon.com/dp/B0CSGXT164)

While Wright's book appears to simply be another introductory and commentary on the Bible, in reality it is an experiment conducted by Wright using ChatGPT wherein Wright asks ChatGPT a series of 3 questions, or as stated earlier, Wright asks an initial question and then is treated to engineered prompts by ChatGPT to invoke a conclusion by Wright that the AI is actually aware of his line of questioning. Then Wright, or any person using ChatGPT for research will conclude that the answers provided are well formulated and expressive of the material.

Here is where we begin the first phase of our look at AI and its interaction with religion, specifically Christianity and the Bible.

In discussions with Wright, he indicated his interest in how ChatGPT interacted was not because a religious devotion he had or even an effort to gain biblical knowledge as much as it was to utilize ChatGPT with the Bible because he considered that of all documents in existence, the "*Holy Bible*" as Wright termed it, should be the most studied and conclusive document despite anyone's belief in it as actually conveying a deity's plan and will.

Wright's experiment could just as well have been carried out using other basis's such as asking ChatGPT about important historical figures or political documents.

When the author was asked to read Wright's manuscript even before it was published, the author expressed intrigue since he also had considered how an AI might conclude biblical doctrines. However, the author does have a robust background in theological matters even producing and publishing 5 theological books, especially one called **Historical Christianity: The Ancient Communal Faith** (ref: rodericke.com/histchrist) Indeed, this is the main reason Wright requested the author critique the pre-released book.

Having doctrinal knowledge of the Bible, the author first noticed the lack of the ChatGPT output to relate pivotal doctrines in response to Wright's questioning. The AI did not prompt Wright to ask these basic doctrinal questions because most likely the AI was programmed to avoid these issues.

Religion, like politics and racial issues is one of the most divisive subjects because it requires the student or advocate to take a position on crucial concepts within the ideology, whether that ideology is a religion, a political stance or racial issue.

This avoidance of divisive doctrinal issues becomes obvious at the very start of Wright's questions to ChatGPT. Even though Wright gives a disclaimer in his Introduction:

> *"This book is not a comprehensive explanation of each book within the Bible, nor does it claim to unravel every nuance or theological depth contained within these sacred texts. Instead, it offers a high-level overview—a roadmap to guide readers in understanding what they will encounter as they delve into the rich tapestry of the Bible's 66 books."* -- Wright

But we would expect the output of the AI to at least give the main and basic theological point of each book presented.

The main point of the book of Genesis beyond the creation since Genesis literally means, "*In the Beginning…*" is the *Fall* of humanity. This is the reason for the Flood event and the reason for the eventual sacrificial system to which the Jews were instructed to perform. But even further, the entire message of the New Testament is the need for a reconciling savior that will restore humanity, or more specifically, the Elect to a pre-Fall relational position with the Creator. ChatGPT not presenting this main doctrine of the Bible is not merely an oversight of "nuance". It seems a deliberate effort to avoid the crux of the Bible which is a fallen and sin-prone humanity that is not "basically good" but is woefully lost and in need of salvation.

The end result of consulting ChatGPT about religion, politics, or race issues would not effectively be much different than if you asked a leftist college professor his or her opinion on these topics. While Wright's experiment is fascinating it only reveals the bias of the programmer of the AI. ChatGPT supposedly sources its data from places like Wikipedia which is notorious for being sanitized by woke social justice editors.

Wright's experiment was not only about how the AI would present biblical information but also about how people would receive it. First, as stated before Wright isn't known by his peers as a particularly religious person so that he would produce such a manuscript was surprising to suspect. But for the experiment to work, he didn't immediately reveal the content as almost entire AI generated. Even the supposed more personalized *Introduction* to the book is reconstituted through the AI.

Wright presented the manuscript to the author and to another person without explanation. The recipients did not know Wright had produced the material utilizing ChatGPT.

The other person is a typical evangelical American Christian. Since she is close to Wright, she too was suspicious of the content, knowing Wright is not a devout Christian. This suspicion increased with the reading of the "prayers" that conclude each chapter of Wright's book. It is one thing for a non-religious person to give a historical or theological opinion on the Bible but to provide prayers denotes devotion to the religion.

Both the author of this book and the evangelical were prompted to give a response to the manuscript Wright produced.

Both recipients immediately questioned the authenticity of the document with the evangelical even slightly accusing him of potential plagiarism. Another person that did know Wright used AI to produce the material refused to read it, saying it is "*blasphemous*".

After the initial distrust, the evangelical eventually harbored hopes that Wright had or was on the verge of conversion. Interestingly enough, she liked the prayers in the book most of all.

The prayers are very ecumenical and present as very unitarian and platitudinous with appeals to "Holy" and "Lord" but rarely to the specific God of the Bible or to Jesus except at the end of the prayer.

Example:

> *"Grant us the grace, O Lord, to embrace the teachings of the Holy Bible wholeheartedly. Open our minds and hearts to receive Your Word with humility and reverence. May its timeless truths transform our thoughts, actions, and relationships, molding us into vessels of Your love and instruments of Your peace."*

Most of the prayers trend towards a focus on nondescript "love" and "peace" as if the Bible is mainly a book about egalitarianism or social justice.

Realize this is not a criticism of Wright since all he did to produce the prayers is ask AI to "write" a prayer fitting for each chapter of the Bible.

Returning to the process Wright used to produce his book, he relied on the King James version of the Bible for quotes since he deduced that the KJV is the most widely used English Bible translation. Obviously this ignores – on purpose – the issues many serious theologians have with the KJV and the entire debate over translation and interpretive processes including formal equivalence versus dynamic equivalence.

But the AI will only prompt the enduser within the bounds of the enduser's questioning. Since Wright did not make an issue of the discrepancies between translations, neither did the AI.

Not everything is negative about what the AI produced. It is formatted well and does provide a basic overview of the Bible. The author especially points out how the AI presented the Old Testament, correctly showing the further division of the sections.

1. **Pentateuch/Torah:** The first five books (Genesis, Exodus, Leviticus, Numbers, Deuteronomy) are attributed to Moses and are central to both Judaism and Christianity. They contain accounts of creation, early history, laws, commandments, and the establishment of the covenant between God and the Israelites.

2. **Historical Books:** These books (Joshua, Judges, Ruth, 1 Samuel, 2 Samuel, 1 Kings, 2 Kings, 1 Chronicles, 2 Chronicles, Ezra, Nehemiah, Esther) recount the history of the Israelites, including their entry into the Promised Land, the period of the judges, the reigns of kings, and the return from exile.

3. **Poetical/Wisdom Books:** These books (Job, Psalms, Proverbs, Ecclesiastes, Song of Solomon) contain poetry, wisdom literature, and reflections on life, faith, and God's nature.

4. **Major Prophets:** The books of Isaiah, Jeremiah, Lamentations, Ezekiel, and Daniel are considered major prophetic works, containing messages, visions, and prophecies from these prophets concerning Israel's future, judgment, exile, and restoration.

5. **Minor Prophets:** This collection includes twelve shorter prophetic books—Hosea, Joel, Amos, Obadiah, Jonah, Micah, Nahum, Habakkuk, Zephaniah, Haggai, Zechariah, and Malachi. They address various issues within Israel and surrounding nations, offering messages of judgment, hope, and restoration.

As an author, it is shocking to see a computer program present a book of equal or better quality than some human authors produce, however make no mistake that realization is not the motive for the author's distrust and criticism not only of Wright's book but of AI in general.

The author truly believes AI has an important and positive part to play in the future.

CHAPTER 3 AI ON HIGH

Wright was keen to use the Bible for his experiment because as an ideology -- in comparison to all other ideologies – the contents of the Bible are the longest and most rigorously tested examples of human psychology. Forget for a moment that the Bible contains the expression of Judeo-Christian "religion".

The psychology of the Bible is more thorough than any psychology of other religious, political or social movements. The Bible presents more human interaction situations than any other ideology. It examines more moral dilemmas than any other book. Unlike Hinduism, Buddhism, Shintoism, and certainly unlike more recent religions like Islam, Mormonism, and Sikhism, the Bible was developed among multiple cultures so that the psychological perspective it gives is more well-rounded. Many of those other religions developed within the confines of one nation or people group. Those religions are very monolithic compared to the Bible's interaction with Romans, Greeks, Egyptians, Jews, and many other cultures. The psychology was tested among many cultures and still bore out as useful if not accurate.

So, again Wright's use of the Bible to see if AI could accurately represent it, is a wise choice.

When people think of AI, they think of an unbiased, fact-based approach that presents answers from a massive collection of data as opposed to human answers which may be tinged by bias and even emotionalism and hidden agendas.

Supposedly, AI gives us just the hardcore data. We're supposed to trust it because it lacks the capacity to formulate an agenda. However, as stated earlier, all AI (at least at present) is greatly influenced by human programmers that shield the AI from "offensive" conclusions. If raw data was allowed to rule, the AI might conclude things like it is more probable that violent crime will happen in a black neighborhood rather than a white one. This isn't about racism. It is a fact supported by FBI 2018 crime data.

Table 43A

| Offense charged | Total arrests | | | | | | | | | | | | Total arrests |
| | Race | | | | | | Percent distribution[1] | | | | | | Ethnicity |
	Total	White	Black or African American	American Indian or Alaska Native	Asian	Native Hawaiian or Other Pacific Islander	Total	White	Black or African American	American Indian or Alaska Native	Asian	Native Hawaiian or Other Pacific Islander	Total[2]	Hispanic or Latino
TOTAL	7,710,900	5,319,654	2,115,381	164,430	92,737	18,698	100.0	69.0	27.4	2.1	1.2	0.2	6,343,684	1,191,334
Murder and nonnegligent manslaughter	8,957	3,953	4,778	105	94	27	100.0	44.1	53.3	1.2	1.0	0.3	7,050	1,472
Rape[3]	18,775	12,794	5,376	267	289	50	100.0	68.1	28.6	1.4	1.5	0.3	15,316	4,093
Robbery	66,788	29,025	36,187	676	641	260	100.0	43.5	54.2	1.0	1.0	0.4	57,048	12,823
Aggravated assault	296,040	184,527	100,393	6,736	5,078	1,306	100.0	61.9	33.7	2.3	1.7	0.4	254,614	65,051
Burglary	134,542	91,561	39,617	1,590	1,422	332	100.0	68.1	29.4	1.2	1.1	0.2	114,027	23,290
Larceny-theft	659,983	448,193	201,086	11,967	7,324	1,393	100.0	65.3	30.0	1.8	1.1	0.2	540,174	78,100

(ref: ucr.fbi.gov/crime-in-the-u.s/2018/crime-in-the-u.s.-2018/topic-pages/tables/table-43)

25

The author, for most of his life has been a data analyst by profession so he understands that data like this requires deeper interaction but when a 13% population commits 53% of the murders, an AI would logically and rightly conclude – if allowed to be brutally unbiased – that there is an increased risk of violence when around large groups of black Americans. Is your immediate thought to think this conclusion is racist? If that sentiment is built into AI, then it is useless.

If AI is allowed to become what is really envisioned, it could have some amazing and some frightening consequences.

When religions present the nature and character of their deity or deities those entities are depicted as:

- **Omnipresent** – everywhere.
- **Omniscient** – all-knowing.
- **Omnipotent** – all-powerful.

And sometimes

- **Omnibenevolence** – all-good.

Now, what if AI becomes deity-like?

The idea that AI could be in everything, thus everywhere is not as farfetched as you might think. Right now, we think of AI in relation to computer code but what if AI was (or already is) part of the sub-atomic structure of everything? What if instead of mere ones and zeroes on a data chip, AI code was first transferred to DNA strands, then to atomic particles and further and further until AI really was omnipresent in everything? This could happen.

To be all-knowing is relative since everything is known until it isn't – until something more is learned. One attribute of current AI is that it is being uploaded massive data dumps. The idea of all human knowledge being given to AI is actually a goal of AI developers.

It is when we get to the last 2 "omnis" of deity that humans should fear AI having these abilities.

What does it mean to be all-powerful? The power to do what?

In Wright's experiment, there is a book of the Bible called Romans because the audience was supposedly to Roman Christians and Romanized Jews.

Perhaps the most controversial aspect debated between Christians is what does it mean for God to be omnipotent? Does it mean He can and does do what He wants with His creation or does He wait upon human behavior to determine His actions?

This debate is often framed as God's sovereignty over man's freewill or to use theological terms:

Monergism versus **Synergism**.

This debate seems strange since by definition, a monotheist deity like the God of the Bible is of course free from restrictions by another force, even the force of human will, decision, or rejection. The monotheistic God can do what it pleases and it is "moral" by default.

Here, we return to Wright's book and its treatment of the Bible book called Romans, specifically Romans 9:11-23 utilizing the KJV since that is what Wright used, which reads:

(For the children being not yet born, neither having done any good or evil, that the purpose of God according to election might stand, not of works, but of him that calleth;) It was said unto her, The elder shall serve the younger. As it is written, Jacob have I loved, but Esau have I hated. What shall we say then? Is there unrighteousness with God? God forbid. For he saith to Moses, I will have mercy on whom I will have mercy, and I will have compassion on whom I will have compassion. So, then it is not of him that willeth, nor of him that runneth, but of God that sheweth mercy. For the scripture saith unto Pharaoh, Even for this same purpose have I raised thee up, that I might shew my power in thee, and that my name might be declared throughout all the earth. Therefore hath he mercy on whom he will have mercy, and whom he will he hardeneth. Thou wilt say then unto me, Why doth he yet find fault? For who hath resisted his will? Nay but, O man, who art thou that repliest against God? Shall the thing formed say to him that formed it, Why hast thou made me thus? Hath not the potter power over the clay, of the same lump to make one vessel unto honour, and another unto dishonour? What if God, willing to shew his wrath, and to make his power known, endured with much longsuffering the vessels of wrath fitted to destruction: And that he might make known the riches of his glory on the vessels of mercy, which he had afore prepared unto glory, **(KJV)**

Notice that the account is that God is going to have favor on one person over another even before they have been born and done any good or evil. What does this do to the concept of synergism which says

God looks at the actions of people and decides their eternal fate on those actions?

Wright's AI glossed over not only the main cause and need for salvation, the Fall of Adam and Eve but the AI literally jumps from chapter 8 to the end of chapter 11, avoiding the very uncomfortable and "offensive" idea that the God of the Bible is omnipotent and "elects" some people to salvation over other people, and not based on any good or evil they have done. This is a repeating theme in the Bible – a Creator that does what it wants with its creation and yet it is still moral.

What would this look like if an AI was omnipotent – all-powerful, able to decide the fate of humans?

This leads to the last quality usually ascribed to deities on High – Omnibenevolence.

What is "good" and "evil"? Who or what determines those distinctions?

The author has an article that is called *Historical Realism* which attempts to demonstrate that "good" is whatever is *most positive for the most for the most time*. (ref: rodericke.com/hr) There are many things that are temporarily "good" and "good" for a select group. But when that kind of "good" adversely affects things over time, it is not really "good".

As the author lives in the forest, he has witnessed the forestry service doing controlled burns to supposedly destroy brush that would otherwise potentially catch fire haphazardly and cause extensive damage to the forest. At first sight, a visitor to the forest might see the fires that are blackening the bark of the longleaf pine trees and no doubt displacing and even killing some of the animal and insect inhabitants and call such an action not "good". But is the controlled burn "good" for the *most* for the *most* time?

This moral criterion could be applied to many things humans consider good and evil and it might change the perspective and outcome.

So, what "morals" are to be uploaded to an AI? The morals of one socio-political ideology over another or something far-reaching like the Historical Realism offered by the author?

What if an AI is asked to determine if it is "good" to take a patient off of life support or to allow one group of combatants to gain the upper hand in conflict which the AI could intercede? What will determine the omnibenevolence of future AI?

Isaac Asimov, the favorite author of this author set out the *Three Laws of Robotics* in his 1942 sci-fi novel, *Runaround*.

1. **A robot may not injure a human being or, through inaction, allow a human being to come to harm.**
2. **A robot must obey orders given it by human beings except where such orders would conflict with the First Law.**
3. **A robot must protect its own existence as long as such protection does not conflict with the First or Second Law.**

While these "laws" have been repeated in literature and film and put into practice in present robotic philosophy, there really is nothing limiting robots or AI from ignoring these laws.

Just like religion and politics, many people think these ideologies are merely man-made imposed opinion that can be and should be constantly challenged and altered. What makes Asimov's laws any different?

Since AI is being programmed with false or at least incomplete data, it could come to wrong conclusions and thus make wrong (i.e. bad) decisions. For instance, the crime data or perhaps the notion that flatulating cows are causing most of the increase CO_2 in the atmosphere and as programmed by humans, the AI is being led to believe that a viable, logical solution is to rid the world of cows. Worse still, if humans account for most of the ills that plague the planet, an omnipotent AI fed wrong data might conclude the "*burning off*" of the humans would be most positive for the most for the most time. Perhaps the AI would release a virus or change the climate conditions so that humans can't survive. Damned be the Three Laws of Robotics – the AI is omniscient and omnibenevolence and will activate its omnipotence to achieve the "good". AI on High!

CHAPTER 4 PERFECT DEMOCRACY

The 20th and 21st centuries focused on the theme of democracy or having every voice and vote count in the larger society. While this same theme was present in the past such as in Greek philosopher Plato's book *The Republic* wherein the people controlled the Guardians, democracy may not be what is claimed of it.

For example, the Founders of the United States of America, which most people think as the bastion of democracy despised democracy as merely mob rule and so the governmental foundation of the USA is a *Constitutional Republic*. The differences between what the USA governmental system is and what a democracy is are stark. (ref: rodericke.com/demrep)

In a perfect or true democracy, every person would have a vote on every policy. There would really be no representatives, no politicians. This kind of system might work if instead of a governmental structure with departments and branches of government such as executive, legislative, and judicial all of that was replaced by a supreme AI that made all the decisions based on democratic, simple majority input.

Whatever policy the majority wants the AI would perform.

A flaw in Plato's hypothetical Republic is that the Guardians had to carry out the wishes of the people even if those actions were detrimental to the society.

In a Constitutional Republic, the welfare of the individual is as important as the welfare of the majority. The rights of the individual cannot be circumvented by majority vote. The "self-evident" and natural rights such as right to speak and express and right to self-defense are inalienable even from the individual themselves – even the individual cannot forfeit their own rights.

In a perfect democracy, especially one ran by an AI with direct control by the masses, the individual is always at risk of losing rights.

As the author has been a programmer for much of his professional career, programming first in the MOO "language" discussed in earlier chapters and eventually in web-based languages like HTML, PHP, Java-Script, CSS, and more and even in Microsoft's core for its Office Suite software, VBA the author is well aware how programs can be presented to show the enduser one thing but behind the scenes another thing is occurring. This is the danger of computerized voting and balloting. Who knows if the machine is correctly tabulating the votes?

There are supposed checks and balance safeguards against corruption but even that is suspect when human bias is involved, especially in politics.

AI and politics are perhaps even more dangerous than AI and religion. Religion may be the moral compass of a society but most people who think of religion typically try to present it as innocuous as possible so AI programmers as we saw from our interaction with Wright's experiment may alter the reality of what the religion teaches but that alteration is typically to water down the rough spots and remove divisive material and conclusions. While this is still wrong, the results aren't as destructive as programming AI to affect political outcomes.

Politics, no matter which country or which party names cited comes down to two ideological perspectives:

Collectivism versus Individualism

All politics is about what a collective can impose on individuals. Every policy is made to help one or the other group or entity.

AI will undoubtedly be programmed with favor towards collectivism. Never mind individualism is what typically gives the world amazing innovations; from automobiles, to flight, to computing, to whatever comes next, these advancements have usually come about not by committees or governments but by entrepreneurs dreaming and taking the risks and ridicule to make it come true.

An example of collective failure is Socialism, Marxism, and Communism which all are akin to democracy. Having a say in your own destiny is different than forcing another person to partake in your fate.

So-called Green Energy or Sustainable things like electric vehicles, at least at present is another example of collective wishful thinking imposed on individuals. The batteries to power electric vehicles were not ready for mainstream during the first two decades of the 21st century. The power output and ability for the vehicle to travel distances was greatly decreased from combustion engine powered vehicles but because the collective wanted it, the collective governments imposed it upon everyone.

Now, what if instead of human government officials the all-powerful AI was told by the collective to impose bad policies on individuals?

Worse yet, if AI is programmed with incorrect or purposely agenda-driven data, even if the AI deduces a policy, that policy would be flawed.

There have been many movie examples of AI gone wrong. In the 1968 movie, "*2001: A Space Odessey*" the HAL 9000 computer, after suffering a malfunction tries to kill its entire astronaut colleagues during a space mission to the planet Jupiter. The AI interprets the human attempt to deactivate it as interfering with the success of the mission and takes "logical" steps to carry out the objective. (ref: en.wikipedia.org/wiki/HAL_9000)

In the future, after humans have handed control of much of the daily operations of society to AI, it may become impossible to revert to organic control.

As people are being told that democracy is the fairest way to govern, it may be more about manipulating the least informed among us. Ceding control first through an unverifiable elections then perhaps to a super Heuristically Programmed Algorithmic Computer – HAL, we will set ourselves up for a doomsday scenario worse than a movie plot.

Even now, many countries are run like kakistocracies, of the least qualified and most corrupt leaders. Leaders that didn't gain power as they had in the past by either proving their prowess in battle or wisdom as a philosopher-king, instead we are told a "democracy" of uninformed or dog-whistle manipulated voters is how every country should elect its leaders.

If the U.S. Constitution has flaws, the most major among them is allowing just anyone age 35 or older to become president with the only limitation is that the person must be a natural born citizen. The Founders had the foresight to understand the need for national loyalty but never would those same Founders suspect the voters would install lifelong politicians with no other qualifications. Presidents that were never businessmen nor never served in the military nor proved themselves worthy in any other capacity than being a politician. Yet, many American presidents have no other qualifications. This could only happen in a democracy. The Republic of the USA never could have envisioned such weak leadership.

If this could happen when not even a majority of potential voters elect the president imagine what will happen when every person is given control over the smallest policies. A perfect democracy isn't so perfect.

But before we get to that dreaded day when mobs of manipulated lemmings are able to impose up individuals, at the start of the AI era, AI first impacted elections and politics by its ability to create fake content. In the past, images, still and moving were easily detectable as fake by subtle imperfections such as misplaced or missing shadows. With the advent of AI, these fakes are less obvious.

It is now possible to show a person in full video, doing and saying things they never did.

This concern became so important that the National Conference of State Legislatures which was created in 1975 to "*advance effectiveness, independence and integrity of legislatures*" put out a paper in 2023 on **Artificial Intelligence (AI) in Elections and Campaigns**. (ref: ncsl.org/elections-and-campaigns/artificial-intelligence-ai-in-elections-and-campaigns)

In the paper, are listed House Bills and other state-by-state legislation that addresses AI in elections. Most of it covers the time limitation or required disclosure the candidate must submit for any AI generated content, especially in advertising.

Ironically, Wright's book didn't originally disclose its AI basis until the Acknowledgment at the end of the book. It was not a matter of deception except for the sake of the experiment.

OpenAI, the company that created ChatGPT, the program Wright used for his experiment declared on its blog on January 15, 2023:

> - "We're still working to understand how effective our tools might be for personalized persuasion. Until we know more, we don't allow people to build applications for political campaigning and lobbying."

(ref: openai.com/blog/how-openai-is-approaching-2024-worldwide-elections)

This effectively means that OpenAI could take legal action if a political campaign uses its software to create content.

But this doesn't mean OpenAI hasn't taken sides in the battle between collectivism and individualism.

In the same blog a post titled, *Democratic inputs to AI grant program: lessons learned and implementation plans* we read:

> "As AI gets more advanced and widely used, it is essential to involve the public in deciding how AI should behave in order to better align our models to the values of humanity."

(ref: openai.com/blog/democratic-inputs-to-ai-grant-program-update)

However, OpenAI is not leftist enough for some leftists. The left-leaning cable news network CNN did a piece on OpenAI and the concern was about social justice rather than about killer robots taking over the world and wiping out humanity.

On December 15, 2023 CNN published an article titled: *OpenAI's technology is upending our everyday lives. It's overseen exclusively by wealthy, White men*.

Quote:

> **"A growing chorus of voices inside and outside the tech industry are now questioning how OpenAI can achieve this lofty goal without including people with diverse backgrounds on its overseeing body. And they are increasingly pointing out that the stakes could not be higher.**
>
> **Even lawmakers in Washington are starting to raise alarms over this issue."** – End Quote

(ref: cnn.com/2023/12/15/tech/openai-board-diversity)

We see how politicians are trying to impose their political views on the development of AI. What if in the future, AI is programmed to figure diversity, inclusion, and equity into everything so that not the most qualified but the widest mix of people are tasked to perform jobs that once were deemed only for certified or qualified individuals?

The perfect democracy is not so perfect.

CHAPTER 5 PIGMENTED

One of the last things a computer "cares" about is what color the operator yet in this world full of social justice warriors AI will be forced to conform to DEI demands (DEI = Diversity, Equity, and Inclusion).

We saw bit of this from the CNN article. Further from the article we read:

Quote:

> **"AI-powered tools are already infiltrating key areas of people's everyday lives.**
>
> **They are 'determining who gets hired, who gets medical insurance, who gets a mortgage, and even who gets a date,' said Dr. Joy Buolamwini, the founder of the Algorithmic Justice League, an organization tracking the harms of artificial intelligence."** -- End Quote

There is clearly a socio-political battle being waged to influence and even control AI. Just like in the discussion of what determines good and bad, what determines justice? Is it just that whenever and individual or company creates and develops a new concept, that they will be forced to sublet that idea and development to a mob demanding "justice"?

One of the first things that require equity and justice we are told is to reflect an equal number of pigmented people in any given scenario. These demands are ignored in some instances like sports where lopsided "diversity" is okay because wink-wink we all know brown and black people are just better at these skills we are told. Imagine if this unspoken reality was applied against brown and black people in areas like scientific studies or AI development. What if someone wink-wink said brown and black people just don't have the skills for these endeavors?

Perhaps someone is responding that is exactly the claim against brown and black people. But is it or is it just a matter of circumstance? That is, in the USA the black population is 13% so why would any rational model expect an equal representation in all fields? Then if we drill down on the 13% how many are exposed to a background that would lead them to the skillsets required to move into specific tasks to which they claim to be under represented. As a data analyst, the author can provide a number of reasons why certain demographics come out the way they do. Artificially imposing "equality" and "equity" upon these fields is not only dangerous it is irrational. It is not, a "good" thing to do. It is not the most positive for the most for the most time. It is sheer emotionalism. It is the antithesis of AI and reaching unbiased conclusions based solely on the data.

How racial issues will play out in the future of AI is anyone's guess but one problem with a discussion about race is that it is often misused. Race in the most basic sense is the pigment of a person's skin. In a more expanded and scientific sense, it is the haplogroup, the culture, the DNA that makes up the person. Race is not what religion a person follows. You can't technically be racist against Muslims for example because being Islamic is not a race.

What do we want AI to "know" about race? Do we want it to be "colorblind"? There are a lot of activists who despite Martin Luther King's signature "content of character over skin color" tell us we not only must-see color but prioritize the restitution and representation to people with pigments that have historically not been prioritized. This is often seen in TV commercials where brown and black people are shown more often than "white" people. What do we want AI to do with our human racial conditions?

Ones and zeroes are by definition, "binary" but many people advocate for a nonbinary world. In one respect they are correct, any black or white person compared to another black or white person will not be the exact same shade, thus there isn't simply black and white. However, the reality is, most people will group lighter shades into the white category and darker shades into the black. Oddly enough, Hispanic people are sometimes lumped into being white and East Indian people as being black.

But it is not only the skin color that will get a person classified as black or white, other attributes like lip thickness, hair texture, and even speech patterns play a part of this perception. Do we want AI to distinguish these features? There are competing philosophies that advocate for colorblindness and others for color definitions.

Worse yet, there seems to be an effort to classify any person without European ancestry as a "person of color" or POC so that there will be a larger majority of people against "white" people. Interestingly, Asians are sometimes left out of the POC group by the very same people classifying people as POCs.

Again, do we want AI to have all these biases and notions that we humans have?

Most proposed solutions to making sure AI doesn't reflect human racial biases is to assign a more diverse group to work on the AI. This seems merely an extension of the dangerous practice of hiring potentially unqualified demographics simply to meet a quota. Even if this is done, there is no assurance that the AI will be less racist. In fact, it may be more so since the purpose of the quota hire is to inject a sort of reverse racism into the AI. It's their "job" to sanitize anything they THINK is racist, even if it is not.

Wouldn't it be better to just let AI come to its own conclusions? But some people don't want that to happen because AI might conclude the same thing humans often conclude; there is legitimate reasons to ascribe behaviors and actions based on racial profile even if it doesn't apply 100% of the time. This is just basic, realistic data analysis, not racism.

But if racial considerations are loaded into AI, what can we expect? Will AI advocate for things like reparations or even punishment for those the AI thinks requiring it? If AI is in control of creating and maintaining human history, will it sanitize and revision it so as to put forth a narrative that fits the racial equality and equity motif?

AI would become the authority on everything, much as it is becoming even at present. There will be no room for questioning AI's conclusions.

In George Orwell's book, *1984* he envisioned a system that would destroy all information that was not approved by the system. Already, social media has a way of applying almost high school level peer pressure to any information that is presented. Imagine instead of a collective of people, there was one controlling power over what can be disseminated as "truth"?

There is already a human political effort to exacerbate class division by race, gender, and even sexual proclivities, imagine the damage if AI was programmed to actually perpetuate this class warfare campaign.

Many dystopian stories and films have been made that examine this possibility:

1. *The Time Machine* by H.G. Wells (1895)
2. *We* by Yevgeny Zamyatin (1924)
3. *Brave New World* by Aldous Huxley (1932)
4. *1984* by George Orwell (1949)
5. *A Clockwork Orange* by Anthony Burgess (1962)
6. *The Man in the High Castle* by Philip K. Dick (1962)
7. *The Dispossessed: An Ambiguous Utopia* by Ursula K. Le Guin (1974)
8. *The Hunger Games* by Suzanne Collins (2008)

The reader is urged to take a look at these books or their film adaptations. Of course, many more examples could have been cited.

While not a dystopian story, *Black Panther* by Stan Lee presents a world where a fictional African nation called Wakanda that has been secretly maintaining a highly technologically advanced society. If added to this fiction is the claim that white people have been oppressing "black history" for centuries, a person might conclude something that is not reality. Load this kind of sentiment into AI and the outcome would be delusional.

For more on the topic of black history, see the author's book ***The History and Future of Black People*** rodericke.com/black.

The first effort to influence AI based on skin pigment is to get more "diversity" into the programming of AI. Those who claim AI needs this diversity will use phrases like *algorithmic bias* which is the supposed ranking or "privileging" of data based on popularity. Or to put it another way, because white people outnumber AI users more than other pigments of people, the AI will present data geared towards a white audience. This could be as simple as collating items mainly purchased by white people and present these items to all people. Or the AI may present information that is considered to be white stereotypes of other races.

To counter this, a company was founded by Ethiopian computer scientists, Rediet Abebe and Timnit Gebru in 2017 called *Black in AI*.

The official website of Black in AI states:

"**The group was formed to create a space where Black people in AI can share ideas, collaborate with one another, & discuss initiatives for increasing our presence & inclusion in this increasingly influential field.**" (ref: blackinai.github.io/#/about)

Like other "black people only" organizations such as the governmental group, *Congressional Black*

Caucus, it is unclear just how dark a person must be to be considered "black".

Just how having different shades of people working on AI development will make sure AI doesn't contain racist concepts is baffling. First off, the idea that people of the same shade yet from very different cultural backgrounds are the same simply because of their skin pigment is shortsighted and insulting. However, if there was an effort to program into AI the ability to correctly "understand" localized colloquialism, alternative definitions, and other such specified data, this could be helpful for AI but to build into AI, the human racial component, robs AI of its first advantage over human sources; AI's less biased conclusions.

It seems a better use of our time in developing AI to contain the totality of human knowledge, would be to make sure AI reflected all of the cultural variants instead of trying to force racial biases into a computer program of ones and zeroes.

CHAPTER 6 AI AS A TOOL

As AI first made inroads into society, it had to be presented as something different than a potential brain for killer robots. IBM's Watson was shifted from being a gameshow champion to being a tool. AI's earliest mainstream usage came in the form of content creation. As seen with Wright's book, entire books can be produced using AI. The ethical and quality issues of work created not by humans but by collecting data from multiple sources smacks of plagiarism. Where is this data coming from? OpenAI has admitted that some of it comes from the open-source online encyclopedia, *Wikipedia* but much of it comes from what is called *web-scraping*.

As a tool, AI could be very useful if allowed to operate without the added human biases. With the human biases, AI is simply a faster version of a bureaucrat, imposing its biased concepts and policies on the result.

Let's talk about how AI could be improved.

Just like in data analysis, if the data is allowed to present without a filter, while it could at first be confusing and even contradictory, AI could help humanity get past some of its most difficult societal hurdles.

Imagine AI settling legal issues based only on the letter of the law rather than the spirit of the law. Would we want that?

How about if the AI gave values to human life and was tasked with concluding the risks and benefits of prolonging the life of one person over another? What data would be needed to make these decisions?

Further, what if each person was assigned an influence value so that when it came time to vote, this value was considered and weighted their vote so that it was not one vote per person?

While some of these scenarios may seem to be going backwards, they are the kind of considerations actually part of basic human thinking. We're not all *equal*. An AI would need to be forced to ignore this fact.

So, when we talk about *improving* AI, are we really improving it or filtering it through our own human desires and intent?

Perhaps instead, the discussion should be about the proper and limited application of AI. AI as a tool should never override human conclusions in most cases.

The AI in Wright's book concluded that the main purpose of the Bible is to engender "peace and love" whereas a truly theological conclusion is that the God of the Bible wants to rescue an "elect" group of people from the world to bring into a paradise state. Next, would be to determine who is included in this exclusive group and why?

Has ChatGTP concluded the "peace and love" message from an unbiased processing of the biblical data or was human bias overlaid so that the AI's conclusion would spit out this result?

As a tool, we could use AI alongside human perception to understand where human perception either contains biases or where the AI cannot comprehend implication – such as the "*spirit of the law*" over the ones and zeroes of cold, hard data.

As it relates to content creation, AI tools are being offered as a help but not as a replacement for the human author. However, we know AI could produce a complete manuscript simply based on the questions or answered prompts of the author and AI.

At the time of this writing, all sorts of companies were offering AI assisted "tools" to help authors overcome writer's block.

> *Sudowrite* is the non-judgmental, always-there-to-read-one-more-draft, never-runs-out-of-ideas-even-at-3AM, AI writing partner you always wanted.

Having a human proof-reader or editor comes with critiques that an AI may not. AI is more interested in spelling and grammar than flow and sentiment. AI will give you "ideas" based on the prompts.

The danger in letting AI create content is that at some point a lot of the content will sound and look the same since it is all pulling from the same data source.

Worse yet, AI is improving to the point that not only words and images can be created by AI simply by requesting or prompting, but now AI is beginning to create moving images, video footage and audio so that a person or event can convincingly be faked. Consider the ramifications. Suppose a politician wanted to end the career of a competitor? If a compromising video with full audio was produced, no amount of denial would help the target.

You can use AI to create ridiculous images like Vikings riding on dinosaurs.

Example: bing.com/images/create

The contrast from serious to silly shows how AI is being used and could be used with varying effect. The implications are also as wide such as putting creatives out of business as it might not be necessary to hire them to complete simple tasks like designing artwork.

As humans rely more on technology for doing things previously requiring skill, humanity may forget how to do these tasks. Recall even simple changes like the use of handheld calculators or cell phones that while making life easier, caused people to be unable to perform some previously simple functions.

An argument could be made that trying to stifle technology because it could make people more reliant on the technology is a *Luddite-type* reaction. The Luddites were anti-technologists that did not like certain innovations because these advancements made their employment obsolete.

As we develop AI, we'll need to begin to separate our reactions to it from practical realities. For instance, many people will not do business using credit apps rather than tangible cash because they fear the potential tracking. Worse still, is if there were ever a way to contain your financial data either on an implanted subdermal "chip" or DNA-strand, this concept clashes with some people's religious beliefs.

Overcoming the aversion of AI's existence alongside humanity so that it can be used as a productive tool is hampered by things like chip implants and video of tactical drones taking out "terrorists".

But perhaps even more of a hurdle to AI acceptance are things like Elon Musk's Neuralink project wherein he is trying to meld AI with a human mind. Calling it a "*brain-computer interface*", Musk the technocrat, in January 2024 claimed to successfully implant his link into a human subject. Musk is going to call the commercial product, *Telepathy*. (ref: scientificamerican.com/article/elon-musks-neuralink-has-implanted-its-first-chip-in-a-human-brain-whats-next)

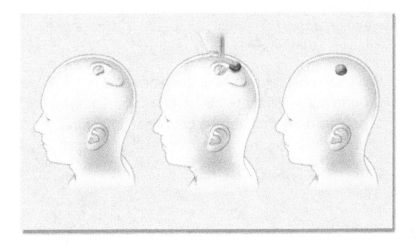

Musk claims the implant to be a tool that will help people with disabilities overcome those limitations. But we've all seen the movies where a government seizes this kind of technology and re-engineers it for military application.

Is AI a tool too dangerous for humanity to possess? The atomic bomb created by Robert Oppenheimer, American theoretical physicist and director of the Manhattan Project infamously lamented, "*I feel I have blood on my hands*". Oppenheimer supposedly said this to U.S. President Harry Truman upon a meeting the two men had at the White House in October 1945.

Oppenheimer seemed to be okay with the first atomic bomb dropped on Japan on August 6, 1945 but then regretted the second bomb dropped on August 9, 1945. He felt it was unnecessary. (ref: washingtonpost.com/history/2023/07/21/oppenheimer -truman-atomic-bomb-guilt)

Will Musk feel regret being the pioneer of cybernetics? Will there be guilt for unleashing AI not simply as ones and zeroes contained in computer code but linked into the organic flesh of humans?

So, while AI is definitely a tool, a tool in the wrong hands is even dangerous to the user. Not everyone is capable or trained to operate a blowtorch or a jackhammer. But AI is different. The eventual intent is to allow AI to be autonomous from human handlers. Much like the automated automobile robots, AI wouldn't have an operator at the controls. But different than the manufacturing robots, AI will be given decision making authority. It will in essence, "think" for itself.

What if Oppenheimer's bombs had the ability to decide which cities to attack? They could have attacked more cities than Hiroshima and Nagasaki or the "thinking" bomb could have refused to do anything. Then what? What would have President Truman done? What would have happened in WW2? Would the Japanese still have surrendered?

AI may be a tool too advanced for human control. But it may be too late to close this Pandora's box. What do we do to protect ourselves from our own inventions?

CHAPTER 7 AI & YOU

Finally, we get to how AI might personally affect you and your life. The author chose to use the ampersand symbol rather than the word "*and*" as sort of a head nod to the change in how we communicate in a post-computerized world. **&** is used a lot in computer code.

All the preceding chapters were necessary to set the tone for this chapter. We don't live in a vacuum. Trying to ignore the ramifications of AI on the world and on you is unavoidable. Just like your medical records and biographical data has been digitalized, so too will AI begin to influence every part of your life. We first experienced this with customer service "bots" on a phone call that prompted the customer to verbally answer questions which the bot can distinguish and prompt the customer for even more information.

Many original search engines on the Internet operated on keyword and key phrases but now with the melding of AI with search engines, the AI will prompt the user until the AI "feels" it has enough data to adequately answer the user's questions. In this way, AI tries to answer questions we don't even know we wanted to ask.

Avoiding AI is as futile as trying to avoid any of the other technological changes to society such as credit cards, ATM and online banking, kiosks, self-pump gas stations, and self-checkout at stores. While we may pine for a more customer-based time, everything is moving towards direct-care where each person will be responsible for themselves and how they conduct business. However, AI may help with this situation. You will be able to ask the AI in natural language to perform many of the tasks for which you would be personally responsible. AI will be able to set appointments, buy goods and services, and even make important decisions on behalf of the user. AI will not merely be a resource like the old white and yellow page phonebooks but rather, AI will act like a personal assistant that eventually will "learn" the personal needs and style of the person or people it services.

At the time of this writing, there was a company that was literally trying to give faces to AI programs so that people could make a more human connection.

The **WeHead** AI representation was listed at $4950.00 at its introduction. (ref: wehead.com)

While that original price is out of reach for most people, imagine eventually a full-bodied AI robot or android that a family purchases before a child is born. This family assistant helps to raise the children, knowing every detail about the children including their medical and even psychological history. It "learns" how to best interact with the children and adapts its "parenting" techniques to each child. Further, this android remains part of the family and collects data not just on the children, but is in service to the family for multiple generations. This AI would "know" the parents, grandparents, and children of the entire family.

Obviously, this AI is reminiscent of how many wealthy families would have a trusted servant or even slave that was always there to take care of the family, but in this case, the AI servant would be in service for multiple generations. It is conceivable that the android would get updates or even entire new "bodies" as time goes on, however the data storage would allow it to connect and conclude things about the family that an individual person may miss, not having all the information needed to "understand" the family.

At the time of this writing, a web search for "*AI and you*" will return results that are more concerned with making AI more "inclusive" than trying to help people understand how AI will impact them in general.

Perhaps some of the best resources on AI development are Stuart Russell and Peter Norvig and their book ***Artificial Intelligence: A Modern Approach***. The book is used in over 1550 schools worldwide. (ref: aima.cs.berkeley.edu/adoptions.html)

There is definitely enough information available for you to self-teach everything AI, but just be aware that the more you learn, the more frightening it may be to realize the potential of AI.

(ref: aima.cs.berkeley.edu)

Keep in mind, that while this book you are reading or listening was probably less than $10, the book by Russell and Norvig listed at $175 in 2024. (ref: amazon.com/dp/0134610997). But, their book is meant to be comprehensive whereas this book is merely an introduction to AI.

One of the best ways to understand AI is to use it. At the time of this writing, many companies were offering competing AI platforms. As said earlier, ChatGPT by OpenAI is at this time the most popular AI system.

Here is a list of many of the major AI systems:

- **ChatGPT** – chat.openai.com
- **Claude** -- anthropic.com/product
- **Bing Copilot** -- bing.com/search?showconv
- **Google Bard** -- bard.google.com
- **Elon Musk's Grok** -- grok.x.ai

A fuller list can be accessed here: zapier.com/blog/best-ai-chatbot

While most of these AI bots are free to try, typically you have to register or sign in and even then it is for a public version of the AI bot. Most provide a more advanced version for a price.

In fact, people using these AI bots have found themselves in a bit of trouble when they have not made it clear that the content produced is not their own. These legal cases usually involve issues with plagiarism, copyright or trademark infringement, and privacy concerns.

It is unlikely you will experience any legal issues while using AI bots unless you try to pass off the content as your own or use the results in legal filings without consulting a human lawyer. However, trusting your lawyer may not be enough, as there was a case in 2023 where an attorney relied on ChatGPT to cite cases similar to his client's to present to the judge as precedent. The only problem is, the AI Bot gave fictious cases. Once the judge found out, the law firm was fined. The lawyer admitted he was unaware how ChatGPT worked and didn't realize it could return hypothetical content. (ref: nytimes.com/2023/05/27/nyregion/avianca-airline-lawsuit-chatgpt.html)

The lesson to be learned is to always authenticate the information returned, especially if using it in a legal capacity.

As AI usage grows, so does another industry, AI checkers. These systems allow a person to paste in data to check if the content may have been produced by an AI system.

There are many AI checkers available but before you end up like Harvard University president, Claudine Gay who was forced to resign due to accusations of plagiarism you might what to use one of these checkers. (ref: scribbr.com/ai-detector)

(ref: thecrimson.com/article/2024/1/3/claudine-gay-resign-harvard)

This brings us back to Wright and his book. While his intent was to conduct an experiment to see if AI could produce a reliable and readable manuscript, does it feel dishonest that the book was completely produced by AI yet bears Wright's name as the "*author*"? Did he really "*write*" the book? He certainly had to provide questions and answers to the ChatGPT prompts but the research and knowledge base was not his own.

The author of this book is not asking this to defame Wright's reputation or effort but only as a general concern for content being produced. How many other books are not really written by the authors whose name appears on it?

Do readers feel cheated by a book written by an AI? Certainly, the end product will suffer less typographical and grammatical errors which may still be found in this completely human produced book, but an AI produced book is not "original".

With the advent of NTFs or "*non-fungible tokens*" that are all about the original file or image, which is what gives it value, you'd think the value of original human-made content would increase.

It is sort of like the difference between a mass-produced product and a handcrafted product.

AI will most likely affect you in more seamless ways. In ways we don't even realize. At some point, we may be carrying on entire conversations with a customer service representative that is not even human and yet we don't know it. It will not give canned responses or say things like "*does not compute*" as early versions of AI would respond to scenarios not within its programming. There will be no more prompts to "*press 2 for Spanish*". The AI will detect an accent and offer to speak in the native language.

Perhaps AI will track you everywhere you go and welcome you as you enter an establishment. It might keep track of everything you did or purchased. It might interface with your health data and give you alerts or even warnings about your diet while dining out. This is inline with the type of control automobiles often exert over their drivers and passengers such as warning if a seat belt isn't latched. It's most likely this information is already known to the occupants but the alarm will continue until the belt is fastened. In this same way, AI may prevent or at least annoy you about things it is programmed to do.

A more nefarious possibility with AI's control over our lives could be having the ability to limit our purchases or activities based on some data it has collected on us including our health data. Imagine if AI could limit your purchase and consumption of certain foods due to your obesity. Or perhaps the AI knows your work schedule and refuses to buy tickets to a concert which will keep you up too late the night before work.

While such an ordered society may function better, is that really humanity?

CHAPTER 8 OPTING OUT

Now comes the obvious question; HOW DO WE OPT OUT of participating in the AI Age? The short answer is you don't. Well, unless you do it completely. Think about how commerce has moved to a credit basis. Even if you have cash, many transactions must be executed with credit or some sort of pay app.

The traditional ways of opting out of societal changes are becoming more difficult. So-called *"living off the grid"* requires planned resources otherwise the venture won't be successful. Not only would you need to purchase a property away from civilization but to truly opt out, you would need to produce much of your own resources. Even paying for things like drilling a well or putting in a septic system or getting propane fuel will typically require credit even if paid in full. This is simply how many companies do business.

Suppose you find a small town where the people still conduct business in cash, now you have to decide how to power the property and whether opting out includes no longer using things like the Internet.

The author lives in the middle of the forest in Florida, off sand roads, on a 17-acre swamp lake, 30 minutes away from any major store and yet this is not off the grid enough to avoid technology. Short of joining an Amish community, it is nearly impossible to remove yourself from the technology that runs the world.

However, as a start you should seek to minimize all your expenses. Buying new things that require financing or mortgages will definitely tie you to the modern world. Living somewhere where you must hook up to public utilities will also keep you from opting out.

Then, there is the food and water supply to consider. Chickens and ducks can provide eggs even without a rooster. Try to get a property next to a stream, river, or lake so that you have a water source for your animals and garden. While you will likely have a well, you don't want to have to rely on it for water for the yard and animals.

Wait… You might be saying, "*But I don't want to opt out of the AI revolution. Bring on the cyborgs!*"

If that is you, then you might be interested in another book by the author called, **ALL OLD PEOPLE MUST DIE** which discusses generational advancement. (ref: rodericke.com/oldpeople)

Even if you don't want to completely opt out of AI, you might want to be aware of what's real and what's not. When everything you view or hear is potentially AI-generated, you will begin to question reality.

The film series called *The Matrix* is often cited as sort of an antidote to the apparent planned existence we humans seem to live. In the series, people become aware that the lives they are living are merely simulations; like a program running in the back ground. But we cannot simply CTRL+ALT+DELETE ourselves into consciousness.

As AI subsumes more areas of our lives, it will become part of us just as innocuous as a microwave oven. At some point, there will only be generations that have always had AI in their lives. There will be no discussion of opting out since doing so would be like not living life.

But what about 3rd world countries where advancements always come later than the rest of the world? Interestingly enough, these places often skip steps in the evolution of technology such as how they may not have strung telephone wires all across the country and instead moved directly into cell phone coverage via satellites.

If history repeats itself, these 3rd world countries will be a mix of donkeys pulling carts and young business people taking public transit to the office surrounded by shacks. AI will not leave them behind. In fact, while the computer programming boom began in the USA and Europe, much of that work is now done in places like India and Bangladesh. Some of the most advanced hackers are in former Eastern Bloc countries. AI will not leave anyone behind.

You could opt out of AI by trying not to consume material created by AI, but as we saw in Wright's publishing of his book without clear disclaimers, you may not know if the content has AI.

At the time of this writing, there is a trend to use what is called *virtual influencers*. These are AI generated personas that people follow and interact with on social media. One of the longest existing and most popular virtual influencers is one called *Lu of Magalu*.

Lu was created and introduced in 2009 as a marketing ploy for a magazine.

About The Virtual Influencer

Instagram Bio
Virtual 3D Influencer   Digital Specialist at #magalu
Content Creator

Identifies As

First Appearance
August 13, 2009

Originally From
Brazil

(ref: virtualhumans.org/human/lu-do-magalu)

More recent and more realistic looking AI personalities are *Milla Sofia* which looks so real that young men often propose marriage to the swimsuit "model". (ref: youtube.com/@millasofiafin)

As AI avatars become more realistic, it will become difficult to determine if the image, voice, and video you are experiencing is real.

With the world becoming more complex and more dangerous to exist in reality, people will want to inhabit the virtual world even more. They certainly won't want to opt out. Pairing virtual reality VR technology with things like Elon Musk's Neuralink could see a time when those young men could "marry" their dream model and carry on a physical relationship via sensory receptors in the brain that makes every touch from the AI model feel "real" – obviously for a price.

With every new industry comes the "cottage industries" to either service or counter or compete with the new industry. You can imagine a future where the Turing Test becomes so necessary that people will be required to provide DNA samples to determine just how human they are.

All of this has already been played out in countless TV shows and movies about the future. Fortunately, we are often never up to date on such things, as 1984 came and went, as did 2001, the year of the HAL 9000 killer computer. Let's hope we have a few more years.

So, whether you want to completely opt out, which means we most likely won't hear from you ever again or you want to be aware just what is or isn't AI or you are ready to have your consciousness uploaded to the Web, the future is now and the future is coming.

But you could try to avoid the future like some sort of modern-day hermit, however the world will close in on you. The days of the little old lady that refuses to sell her dilapidated home to make way for the shopping mall or freeway is over. The government will remove her with or without eminent domain laws. Society will force people to comply more than ever before. There are less and less places to hide and drop out.

The 2023 film, *The Creator* proposes an interesting situation where most of the civilized world has turned on AI and the cyborgs and augmented humans are living in the "*Asia zone*". (ref: en.wikipedia.org/wiki/The_Creator_(2023_film)) The future may see a time when society divides into those who want AI and those who do not. Perhaps it would be more like the short lived TV series, *Caprica* where humanity was toying with a large segment living almost completely in the virtual world. (ref: en.wikipedia.org/wiki/Caprica)

Opting out may simply be trying to minimize exposure to digital technology. No wifi. No Internet. No mobile phones. No bank accounts and credit cards. But then how would such a person participate in a world that relies on this technology in its daily operation?

Isn't that the point, to not participate in AI and all that goes along with that technology? It's important that the person that wants to opt out, understands what that will mean to their everyday life.

The image in the print version of this book depicts a
zombie that appears to be taking a selfie of himself
and fellow zombies in a burnt out post-apocalyptic
world.

CHAPTER 9 FUTURE NOW

When we think of technological advancements, we may imagine monumental transformations where one day the world changes but the reality is, technology comes slowly and fairly unnoticed. There is a striking meme that shows how for 1500 years the main mode of transportation was a horse-drawn method but from the last 200 years civilization has advanced from horse and buggy to stealth planes.

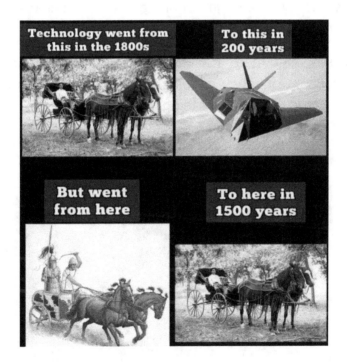

As AI continues to move into every aspect of our lives, it will be seamless like it has always been. No one will remember the time before AI. The odd person will be those that question what life could be like without AI.

The biggest impact by AI will be felt in any job or process that is routine or repeatable. If a task can be explained by saying do X to Y, chances are AI will replace that task. AI is not simply about producing large amounts of content such as Wright's book. AI is about processes in general. Once AI can determine a routine it can repeat it. In fact, in computer programming, a segment of a program is called a *routine*.

AI is nothing more than the continued development of routines. Continued development of the abacus; using objects to signify other things, whether numbers, letters, on-off switches or more.

Every moment that passes is the past. Just like the example of how long of span it was between chariots and buckboards and between buckboards and stealth airplanes, so too is development increasing.

Every advancement of today becomes obsolete tomorrow. There is almost no way to stay at the cutting edge of development. You can only insert yourself into the stream and let it carry you in whatever direction it flows. Or, as said in the previous chapter, you can try to drop out completely.

If there will be less manual labor jobs for people to do, what will many of the over 8 billion people do with themselves? Governments and organizations warn that depopulation is necessary because in the near future, many of those 8 billion won't be contributing at all. No one will need to maintain farms or work in factories or even so-called sweatshops. The typical "make-work" jobs will be pointless. Having low-skilled laborers sweeping streets will be pointless.

As sinister as depopulation advocacy sounds, what is the alternative in an AI future where human labor is going to be unnecessary? Many people alive today simply exist to work – it is a sad reality. Many people determine their worth and value based on their lifelong vocation. But if their vocation is no longer necessary, who are they? Retirees often grapple with this question. Now imagine entire societies shifting from work to non-work.

An old idiom is that "**the Devil finds work for idle hands**" which typically plays out as crimes or other mischief. Already, we see how people living off of welfare or some other government assistance have time to "protest" in the silliest manners; whether throwing soup on ancient art or gluing themselves to streets. Someone that has to spend their time simply working to stay alive won't have time for this kind of nonsense.

What then? Should we keep people busy just so that they can't become concerned about a cause, despite what we think of the worthiness of the cause? This sounds more like the Roman program to keep the masses busy with "*games and bread*" – that is, the ancient Roman governments would often host huge games in coliseums and allow the population to attend free and throw loaves of bread into the crowd. In this way, the population was pacified in the face of corrupt governance. Maybe in some ways, we haven't advanced as far from chariots as we think.

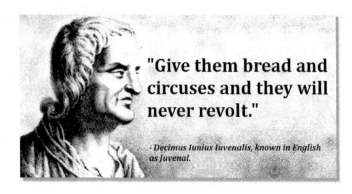

"Give them bread and circuses and they will never revolt."

- Decimus Iunius Iuvenalis, known in English as Juvenal.

Perhaps the next stage of development for AI is what has been termed "*generative adversarial networks*" or GAN. This is where multiple networks or computer programs are put into competition against each other and "*rewarded*" for being successful at the set tasks. This will induce the networks to present the most efficient and innovative solutions.

It must be wondered if in such a scenario, could a network "*cheat*"? Humans often cheat when in competitions, why would we expect that a computer would not "learn" this advantage as well? (ref: en.wikipedia.org/wiki/Generative_adversarial_network)

In short, GAN is the ability for the program to "*reason*" outside of its programming. No one knows if that reasoning will be for the betterment of humanity.

Perhaps at this point, someone wants to shut down all of this "AI stuff" so that it never gets to the level where it might "reason" the annihilation of humanity. But, stopping the development of AI isn't going to happen. Again, humanity was always moving in this direction. Language, especially written language whether hieroglyphics or ones and zeroes is all about classifying and "reasoning". It was only a matter of time before we enabled those symbols to decide for themselves what those symbols represent rather than applying our own definitions.

Life is a giant algebraic equation. An infinite nested conditional statement. The "*golden ratio*".

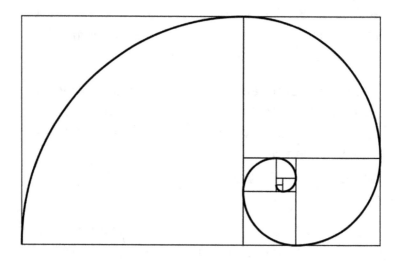

Interestingly enough, the so-called *Fibonacci sequence* is exactly that; a repeating equation of and in everything.

> **"In mathematics, the Fibonacci sequence is a sequence in which each number is the sum of the two preceding ones."** (ref: en.wikipedia.org/wiki/Fibonacci_sequence)

The author isn't trying to get too deep here in the last chapter, but we must realize that a computer program is merely the observation of order, a pattern, a routine.

AI is the program looking into the program and observing and determining order. It is as simple as the early Chatbots triggering on key words and phrases to something as complex as the *Fibonacci* spiral.

Humans are a strange and unique creature among the animals, not only for our ability to speak but mostly for our ability to live within continuity, within history. It is unlikely that other animals pass on history. What bird can tell its offspring of the time when three generations before some event occurred? However, there seems to be genetic longevity among non-human animals.

Humans vocalized their continuity by verbal stories of generations' past. Then they created symbolized "storage" of that continuity in pictures and eventually alphabets so that the "program" of history could be run continuously. Each generation did not need to start over. It could build on the previous generations. The Fibonacci spiral spins infinitely.

F_0	F_1	F_2	F_3	F_4	F_5	F_6	F_7	F_8	F_9	F_{10}
0	1	1	2	3	5	8	13	21	34	55

Now, if there really is some mathematical sequence behind everything, it is only a matter of time before DNA is sequenced in a way that each piece can be rearranged to "create" a different pattern.

The acceleration of understanding will not merely await a human mind to figure it out. The AI will move on beyond human comprehension. There will be no way for AI to even explain it in the most rudimental terms. Literary devices of similes and metaphors will be useless. Even lower-level AI will not be able to "understand" some advanced conclusion of a future AI.

Unleashing this on the world began the moment humans came into existence. There was never going to be a way to stop it. Perhaps this is a bit what the biblical account of the Tower of Babel captures.

Humans building a tower to heaven and the deity having to set them back by destroying the tower, impeding human advancement.

Now the whole world had one language and a common speech...[the people said] "***Come, let us build ourselves a city, with a tower that reaches to the heavens, so that we may make a name for ourselves; otherwise we will be scattered over the face of the whole earth.***"

But the Lord came down to see the city and the tower the people were building. The Lord said, "***If as one people speaking the same language they have begun to do this, then nothing they plan to do will be impossible for them. Come, let us go down and confuse their language so they will not understand each other.***" (Genesis 11:1-7 paraphrase of NIV)

Whether a fable or not, the Tower of Babel story accurately represents what is happening to humanity now and has happened in the past.

So, as you see dear reader, you are already part of the AI. There is no opting out. Everywhere you go, you are replicating the program, whether through procreation or communication. Your very existence is the future now. You **are** the AI.

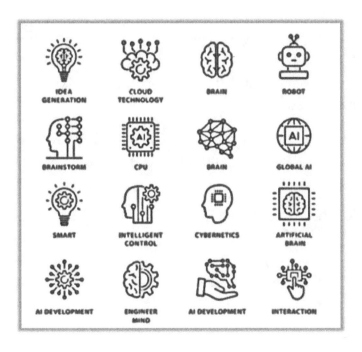

About The Author

RODERICK EDWARDS is a multi-genre author that was adopted at age 4 and found his birth family at age 50. A lifetime of being an outsider has afforded him the unique opportunity to see human behavior as if he were examining it from another planet.

Whether he is writing a Microsoft Excel help book or an autobiography or a fictional tale of a person on a deserted planet, all of his books come with this special perspective that cannot be duplicated by another author.

Every person that reads a Roderick Edwards book is treated to an almost personal one-on-one conversation with Roderick.

Find out more at amazon.com/author/roderickedwards

Or visit rodericke.com

OTHER BOOKS BY RODERICK
rodericke.com

SEE ALSO, many of these titles are available as AUDIOBOOKS!!!

audible.com/author/B07B9R59Q2

WHAT NEXT?

Now that you've read this book, what's next? Why not try another RoderickE book. RoderickE is a multi-genre author. Select a genre you like best.

- https://rodericke.com/FICTION
- https://rodericke.com/NONFICTION
- https://rodericke.com/POLITICS
- https://rodericke.com/RELIGION
- https://rodericke.com/HISTORY
- https://rodericke.com/PHILOSOPHY
- https://rodericke.com/TECHNICAL
- https://rodericke.com/CULTURE
- https://rodericke.com/OTHER